REAL WORLD
MATHS

Extreme
SPORTS

by Wendy Clemson, David Clemson,
Oli Cundale, Laura Berry, and Matt King

Tick

Bristol Libraries

An Hachette UK Company
www.hachette.co.uk
Copyright © Octopus Publishing Group Ltd 2013

First published in Great Britain in 2013 by
TickTock, an imprint of Octopus Publishing Group Ltd,
Endeavour House, 189 Shaftesbury Avenue, London WC2H 8JY.
www.octopusbooks.co.uk

A CIP record of this book is available from the British Library.

ISBN 978 1 84898 916 0

Printed and bound in China

10 9 8 7 6 5 4 3 2 1

With thanks to our consultants: Jenni Back and Liz Pumfrey from the NRICH Project,
Cambridge University and Debra Voege.

WENDY CLEMSON

Wendy is experienced in working with and for children, and has been writing full-time since 1989. Her publications, which now exceed one hundred, have been written for children and sometimes their parents and teachers. In her many maths books, the aim is always to present the reader with challenges that are fun to do.

DAVID CLEMSON

David has wide-ranging experience as a writer and educationalist. His publications list is prodigious. In collaboration with Wendy, David has worked on many maths books for children. He is fascinated by maths and logic puzzles and is keen for the reader to enjoy them too.

WARNING

This book is not intended to be a training manual for the sports of skateboarding, snowboarding or inline skating. If you would like to try any of the sports featured in this book, wear the correct protective clothing and take some lessons from a professional instructor before attempting tricks on a skateboard, snowboard or pair of skates.

The extreme tricks and stunts featured in this book have been performed by professional, highly experienced sportsmen and sportswomen. Read about the tricks and stunts, say, 'WOW', but under no circumstances try them yourself! If you do, don't blame us – **WE TOLD YOU NOT TO TRY IT!**
(Neither the publisher nor the authors shall be liable for any bodily harm or damage to property whatsoever that may be caused or sustained as a result of conducting any of the activities featured in this book.)

CONTENTS

NUMERACY WORK COVERED IN THIS BOOK:

CALCULATIONS:
Throughout this book there are opportunities to practise **addition, subtraction, multiplication** and **division** using both mental calculation strategies and pencil and paper methods.

NUMBERS AND THE NUMBER SYSTEM:
- COMPARING NUMBERS: pg. 7
- DECIMALS: pgs. 10, 26
- FRACTIONS: pgs. 18, 26
- NEGATIVE NUMBERS (on a number line/temperature scale): pgs. 26, 27
- ORDERING NUMBERS: pgs. 10, 26
- ROUNDING: pg. 7

SOLVING 'REAL LIFE' PROBLEMS:
- CHOOSING THE OPERATION: pgs. 17, 18, 24
- MONEY: pg. 24
- TIME: pgs. 15, 17, 19

HANDLING DATA:
- BAR CHARTS: pg. 6
- BAR LINE CHARTS: pg. 13
- PICTOGRAMS: pg. 14
- TALLY CHARTS: pg. 25
- USING TABLES/CHARTS/DIAGRAMS: pgs. 10, 12
- VENN DIAGRAMS: pg. 22

MEASURES:
- AREA: pg. 23
- PERIMETER: pg. 23
- RELATIONSHIPS BETWEEN UNITS OF MEASUREMENT: pgs. 11, 26
- SCALES (reading from a scale): pg. 27
- USING METRIC/IMPERIAL MEASUREMENTS: pgs. 7, 11, 13, 18, 19, 20
- VOCABULARY (time): pgs. 15, 17, 19

SHAPE AND SPACE:
- 2-D SHAPES: pg. 22
- ANGLES: pgs. 8, 9
- LINE SYMMETRY: pg. 21

Supports the maths work taught at Key Stage 2

HOW TO USE THIS BOOK

Maths is important in the lives of people everywhere. We use maths when we play a game, ride a bike, go shopping – in fact, all the time! Everyone uses maths when they take part in sport. You may not realise it, but extreme sportsmen and sportswomen use maths to perform tricks and win competitions! With this book you will get the chance to try lots of exciting maths activities using real life data and facts about extreme sports. Practise your maths and numeracy skills and experience the thrill of what it's really like to be a top extreme athlete.

This exciting maths book is very easy to use – check out what's inside!

Fun to read information about skateboarding, inline skating and snowboarding.

SNOWBOARDING with Laura

Laura says, 'Snowboarding is exciting, fun and gives me a buzz! I get the chance to travel all over the world, meet new people and make new friends. As long as everybody is having fun, snowboarders of all abilities will ride together, offering each other encouragement and helping each other progress and improve. I personally love to ride anywhere that has *big air jumps*, *super-pipes* and technical rails. Snowboarding competitions can take place on mountains, at indoor snow slopes and on dry slopes. There are lots of different types of snowboarding competitions – *Pipe, Big Air, Snowboarder-cross* and *Slopestyle*.'

MATHS ACTIVITIES

Look for the
GO FOR IT! CLIPBOARDS.
You will find real life maths activities and questions to try.

To answer some of the questions, you will need to collect data from a DATA BOX. Sometimes, you will need to collect facts and data from the text or from charts and diagrams.

Be prepared! You will need a pen or pencil and a notebook for your workings and answers.

GO FOR IT!

It is the final of a *halfpipe competition*. **Halfpipes** are like a giant pipe that has been cut in half. They are made of snow. Snowboarders ride down the pipe performing tricks. They are awarded points out of 10 in four categories. The rider with the highest total score is the winner.

In the DATA BOX you will see the scores for six halfpipe finalists.

1) Who got the lowest total score?
2) Who did better than Rob in both **amplitude** and overall impression?
3) Who got the same score as Zak?
4) How many people had total scores that were odd numbers? What were their scores?
5) Who got the highest score and won the halfpipe competition?

(You will find TIPS to help you with these questions on page 28)

A snowboarding halfpipe

The lip

SNOWBOARDING FACT

In *snowboarder-cross*, riders race downhill around and over obstacles in groups of six. Courses can be nearly a kilometre in length. The fastest rider in each group goes through to a final. First rider to the bottom in the final wins gold! In *slopestyle*, competitors take three runs down a course filled with rails, jumps and quarterpipes.

Fun to read facts about EXTREME sports.

12

DATA BOX

If you see one of these boxes, there will be important data inside that will help you with the maths activities.

HAVE FUN, BUT STAY SAFE!

It's easy for extreme athletes to hurt themselves if they don't follow these important safety rules:

- Wear a helmet at all times and make sure it fits snugly.
- Wear knee pads, elbow pads and gloves or wrist guards.
- Take some lessons – a qualified instructor will make sure you know what you are doing!
- Never try a trick that is above your level – start small and build up slowly.
- Always try these sports with friends. It's more fun and if one of you gets injured, someone can go for help.

MATHS ACTIVITIES

Feeling confident? Try these extra **CHALLENGE QUESTIONS.**

IF YOU NEED HELP...

TIPS FOR MATHS SUCCESS

On pages 28 – 29 you will find lots of tips to help you with your maths work.

ANSWERS

Turn to pages 30 – 31 to check your answers.
(Try all the activities and questions before you take a look at the answers.)

GLOSSARY

On page 32 there is a glossary of extreme sports words and a glossary of maths words. The glossary words appear **in bold** in the text.

DATA BOX **HALFPIPE SCORES** (POINTS OUT OF 40)

NAME	STANDARD AIRS	ROTATIONS	AMPLITUDE	OVERALL IMPRESSION
Lyn	5	9	8	4
Rob	8	8	7	8
Ahmed	6	9	6	9
Laura	9	8	8	7
Zak	7	7	8	9
Alli	8	5	5	5

- *STANDARD AIRS*: Tricks and movements such as grabs.
- *ROTATIONS* (spins and flips): 180˚, 360˚ (a full spin), 540˚, 720˚, 900˚, 1080˚, 1260˚.
- *AMPLITUDE*: The height the rider reaches above the lip of the pipe.
- *OVERALL IMPRESSION*: Style, level of difficulty of tricks, creativity and landings.

SNOWBOARDING FACT

The highest *Big air* ever achieved was 9 metres above the lip of the halfpipe. The biggest spin that has ever been done on a jump, is a *1260* (that's 1260 **degrees** – three and half full spins while in the air).

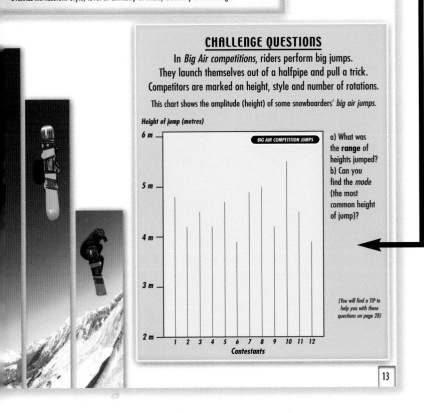

CHALLENGE QUESTIONS

In *Big Air competitions*, riders perform big jumps. They launch themselves out of a halfpipe and pull a trick. Competitors are marked on height, style and number of rotations.

This chart shows the amplitude (height) of some snowboarders' *big air jumps.*

Height of jump (metres)

BIG AIR COMPETITION JUMPS

Contestants

a) What was the **range** of heights jumped?
b) Can you find the *mode* (the most common height of jump)?

(You will find a TIP to help you with these questions on page 28)

13

IT'S EXTREME!

Skateboarding, inline skating and snowboarding are extreme sports. The highly skilled athletes who take part in these sports are able to perform amazing, yet dangerous, moves that seem impossible to you and me! In this book you will read about all the top tricks and the most breathtaking extreme stunts. Who can jump the highest, who can fly through the air the furthest and who can reach mind-blowing speeds. Check out these sports with our boarders and skaters, Oli, Laura and Matt, and decide which sport YOU think offers the most EXTREME thrills.

GO FOR IT!

A group of skateboarders, skaters and snowboarders were asked how often they take part in their sport. Here is a **bar chart**, showing the results.

1) How many people do you **estimate** take part in their sport every day?

2) How many people do you estimate take part more than once a week?

3) Estimate the total number of people who do their sport *once a week* and *at least once a month*?

4) Which of these pieces of information can you find out from the bar chart?
 • The number of boys or girls taking part in extreme sports.
 • The number of 14 year olds.
 • Which days of the week were most popular.
 • The total number of people questioned.

(You will find a TIP to help you with this activity on page 28)

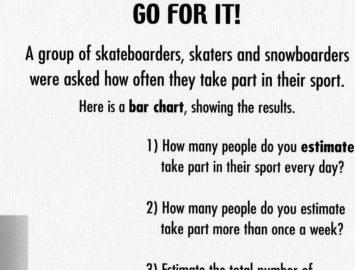

Backside *boardslide down a handrail.*

MONEY FACT

Top professional skaters and boarders can win prize money in extreme sports competitions. Many **pros** are also paid by a company to endorse (use and promote) that company's products, such as skates, boards, clothes, shoes, hats, helmets, sunglasses or goggles.

STREET SKATING FACT

Street skating is exactly what it says – using everyday obstacles, that you see on the street, to help you perform amazing tricks. Skateboarders and inline skaters ride off curbs, over park benches and even down stairs and handrails!

VERT SKATING FACT

Vert skating is all about going up! Vert is short for vertical. Skateboarders and inline skaters perform flips, spins, grabs and slides on ramps or in bowls and **halfpipes**. Vert skaters go to skateparks or build vert ramps.

Snowboarder, Laura Berry rides a rainbow rail.

A 'Japan air' on a halfpipe.

CHALLENGE QUESTIONS

You are preparing for a snowboarding trip and need to choose a new board.

Snowboards come in different sizes to suit the rider's weight, ability and style of riding.

Here are some snowboard designs. You will see the range of lengths each design comes in and the boards' prices.

Compare the different designs:

Board A
Length range: *140–155 cm*
Price: *£299*

Board B
Length range: *147–159 cm*
Price: *£349*

Board C
Length range: *148–156 cm*
Price: *£325*

Board D
Length range: *147–157 cm*
Price: *£343*

a) Which board offers the biggest **range** in length?

b) Which board costs £350 when rounded to the nearest ten pounds?

(You will find a TIP to help you with question b on page 28)

SKATEBOARDING with Oli

Oli says, 'Skateboarding is more than just a sport – there's a whole culture based around it, with companies dedicated to producing clothes, shoes and videos for skateboarders. Skateboarding can give you an enormous sense of satisfaction, and it's also a great way to meet new people. Skateboarding is a very technical and skilful sport, and there are hundreds of tricks to learn. To be a good skateboarder, you need to be athletic and creative. The best skateboarders also have plenty of nerve and lots of dedication, because many top tricks can take years of practice to get right!'

GO FOR IT!

Here are three skateboard tricks.

What **fraction** of a whole turn has the skateboarder made in each trick and how many **degrees** are there in the **angle** of the turn?

POWERSLIDES (tricks 1 and 2):
You shift your weight to one side of the board and slide the back wheels around into a sort of skid. This is a good way of slowing down.

SHOVE-IT (trick 3):
Do an *Ollie*, and while you are in the air, spin the board around underneath you.

(You will find TIPS to help you with these questions on page 28)

Trick 1)

Left foot Right foot

Left foot Right foot

Start position   Finish position

Trick 2)

Start position   Finish position

Trick 3)

Head   Head

Tail   Tail

Start position   Finish position

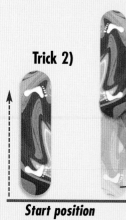

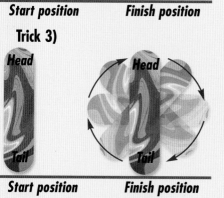

SKATEBOARDING FACTS

The basis for most skateboarding tricks is the *Ollie*, which was invented in the late 1970s by Alan 'Ollie' Gelfand. A skateboarder stomps on the tail of their board with their back foot. As the tail hits the ground, the skater hops up off that foot into the air – the board comes too! The skater then pushes forward with their front foot, levels the board and drops to the ground. Skateboarders can pull *Ollies* over a metre high, and it looks as though the board is actually stuck to their feet!

TRICK TALK

AIR "To air" is to jump into the air with a skateboard.

FAT (also *phat*) This describes a skateboarding trick that is performed over a long distance or to a great height.

FLIP When your board completely flips over and lands back on the wheels.

GOOFY If you skate or snowboard with your right foot forward.

KICKTURN Performed on a **halfpipe**, the skateboarder rotates on the rear wheels of the board with the front wheels raised up from the ground.

MANUAL Travelling on your board, balancing on just the rear wheels —a *wheelie*.

REGULAR If you skate or snowboard with your left foot forward.

REVERT Finishing a trick coming out forwards, then quickly sliding round 180 **degrees** to come out backwards.

SKETCHY When someone is wobbly and just about lands a trick, the trick is *sketchy*.

SLAM Falling off your skateboard and hurting yourself!

SWITCHSTANCE Skating or snowboarding in the opposite stance (regular or goofy) to the one you normally use.

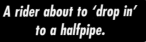

A rider about to 'drop in' to a halfpipe.

CHALLENGE QUESTIONS

This skateboard wheel has made parts of a whole turn.

How many degrees in each?

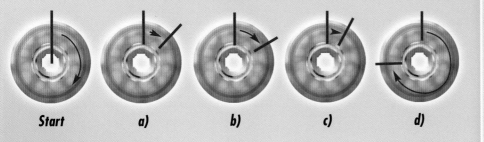

Start   a)   b)   c)   d)

INLINE SKATING with Matt

Matt says, 'Inline skating offers the **adrenaline** rush of high speeds and the thrill of performing tricks and stunts. Speed skaters hurtle around racetracks, while **aggressive skaters** perform jumps, spins and grabs on street courses or vert ramps. *Aggressive skating* or *rolling* was started in the early 90s by a group of extreme sports enthusiasts who each felt their current sport just didn't offer the kind of adrenaline rush they were looking for. Aggressive skating offers incredible thrills and it's also really convenient for beginners because your skates are attached to your feet so, unlike a skateboard, they can't go flying off during a trick!'

GO FOR IT!

Successful speed skaters combine high levels of fitness with good technique and tactics. In sprint races, groups of up to 10 skaters race to qualify for a final. It takes a lot of skill to skate at high speeds in close proximity to the other competitors.

In the final of a 300 metre sprint race there were 10 skaters. Use their times in the DATA BOX to answer these questions:

1) How many skaters had a time under 26 seconds?
2) Which skaters had a time over 27 seconds?
3) If another skater finished the sprint in 25.3 seconds, where would he be ranked, 3rd, 11th or 5th?
4) Three racetracks are holding qualifying races in the first round of a speed skating competition.

- At TRACK A, 209 skaters have entered.
- At TRACK B, 92 skaters have entered.
- At TRACK C, 165 skaters have entered.

If there is a maximum of 10 skaters in a race, how many first round qualifying races will there be at each location?

(You will find some information about PUTTING NUMBERS IN ORDER on page 28)

A speed skater

SPEED SKATING FACT

Matt King has actually been caught speeding on his skates in London! In a daring stunt, performed on empty roads in the middle of the night, Matt and some friends actually managed to set off a speed camera. To build up their speed at the start of their run, the skaters held onto the back of a sports car. They were photographed by the speed camera travelling at 80 mph!

For a fast, fun night out, hundreds of inline skaters in cities, such as London, Paris and New York, gather together to *night skate* and see the city. Marshals travel with the skaters to keep everyone under control.

DATA BOX
SPEED SKATER TIMES

NAME	TIME IN SECONDS
Jolly	25.0
Paul	24.4
Mo	25.2
Josh	27.9
Dec	25.6
Phil	26.3
Ant	30.2
Ian	24.7
Flo	26.8
Dave	31.5

An aggressive skater pulls a big 'mute air' on a ramp.

TRICK TALK

AIRS can be performed both on street courses and vert ramps. While *airing*, skaters perform spins, flips and grabs (grabbing their skates).

FLY FISH The right hand grabs the right boot and extends the leg, while the left foot stays tucked under the body.

MUTE AIR With the legs tucked up in front of the body, the skater reaches their right hand over both shins to grab the left boot.

ROCKET AIR Both legs are extended out in front of the body. The left hand reaches to touch the right toe, or right hand to left toe.

SAFETY GRAB Knees are tucked up so the body is in a ball, right hand on right boot, or left hand on left boot.

LUI KANG Knees to chest, left hand to left foot or right hand to right foot, then the free leg kicks out.

SKATE TALK

FACE PLANT or BAILS When your nose hits the pavement before your hands!

RASPBERRY The *road rash* you get when your skin scrapes the road or pavement.

PAVEMENT INSPECTORS Skaters who are beginners!

CHALLENGE QUESTION

An aggressive skater pulls an *air* on a **halfpipe** and reaches a height of 4 metres.

What is this height approximately in feet?
5 feet   13 feet   23 feet

(You will find a TIP to help you with this question on page 28)

Laura says, 'Snowboarding is exciting, fun and gives me a buzz! I get the chance to travel all over the world, meet new people and make new friends. As long as everybody is having fun, snowboarders of all abilities will ride together, offering each other encouragement and helping each other progress and improve. I personally love to ride anywhere that has *big air jumps, super-pipes* and technical rails. Snowboarding competitions can take place on mountains, at indoor snow slopes and on dry slopes. There are lots of different types of snowboarding competitions – *Pipe, Big Air, Snowboarder-cross* and *Slopestyle*.'

GO FOR IT!

It is the final of a *halfpipe competition*. **Halfpipes** are like a giant pipe that has been cut in half. They are made of snow. Snowboarders ride down the pipe performing tricks. They are awarded points out of 10 in four categories. The rider with the highest total score is the winner.

In the DATA BOX you will see the scores for six halfpipe finalists.

1) Who got the lowest total score?
2) Who did better than Rob in both **amplitude** and overall impression?
3) Who got the same score as Zak?
4) How many people had total scores that were odd numbers? What were their scores?
5) Who got the highest score and won the halfpipe competition?

(You will find TIPS to help you with these questions on page 28)

A snowboarding halfpipe

The lip

SNOWBOARDING FACT

In *snowboarder-cross*, riders race downhill around and over obstacles in groups of six. Courses can be nearly a kilometre in length. The fastest rider in each group goes through to a final. First rider to the bottom in the final wins gold! In *slopestyle*, competitors take three runs down a course filled with rails, jumps and quarterpipes.

HALFPIPE SCORES (POINTS OUT OF 40)

NAME	STANDARD AIRS	ROTATIONS	AMPLITUDE	OVERALL IMPRESSION
Lyn	5	9	8	4
Rob	8	8	7	8
Ahmed	6	9	6	9
Laura	9	8	8	7
Zak	7	7	8	9
Alli	8	5	5	5

- *STANDARD AIRS*: Tricks and movements such as grabs.
- *ROTATIONS* (spins and flips): 180°, 360° (a full spin), 540°, 720°, 900°, 1080°, 1260°.
- *AMPLITUDE*: The height the rider reaches above the lip of the pipe.
- *OVERALL IMPRESSION*: Style, level of difficulty of tricks, creativity and landings.

SNOWBOARDING FACT

The highest *Big air* ever achieved was 9 metres above the lip of the halfpipe. The biggest spin that has ever been done on a jump, is a *1260* (that's 1260 **degrees** — three and a half full spins while in the air).

CHALLENGE QUESTIONS

In *Big Air competitions*, riders perform big jumps.
They launch themselves out of a halfpipe and pull a trick.
Competitors are marked on height, style and number of rotations.

This chart shows the amplitude (height) of some snowboarders' *big air jumps*.

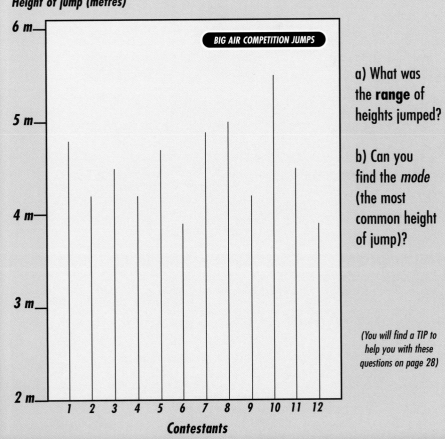

Height of jump (metres)

BIG AIR COMPETITION JUMPS

Contestants

a) What was the **range** of heights jumped?

b) Can you find the *mode* (the most common height of jump)?

(You will find a TIP to help you with these questions on page 28)

13

Many top extreme athletes actually turned professional while they were still at school, and they are now able to make a living from their sport. However, to keep their places at the top, some professionals practise for up to eight hours every day! Oli, Laura and Matt all agree that the only way to get to grips with all the most impressive tricks and jumps, is to practise, practise and then practise again. If you want to be the best, the only way is to put the hours in. Of course, if you love your sport, the more time you can spend on your board or skates, the better!

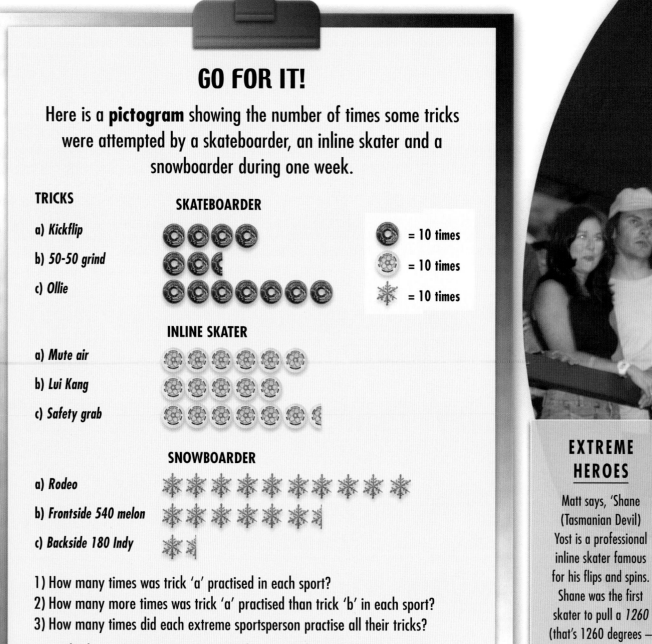

GO FOR IT!

Here is a **pictogram** showing the number of times some tricks were attempted by a skateboarder, an inline skater and a snowboarder during one week.

TRICKS

SKATEBOARDER

a) *Kickflip*

b) *50-50 grind*

c) *Ollie*

⬤ = 10 times

⚙ = 10 times

❄ = 10 times

INLINE SKATER

a) *Mute air*

b) *Lui Kang*

c) *Safety grab*

SNOWBOARDER

a) *Rodeo*

b) *Frontside 540 melon*

c) *Backside 180 Indy*

1) How many times was trick 'a' practised in each sport?
2) How many more times was trick 'a' practised than trick 'b' in each sport?
3) How many times did each extreme sportsperson practise all their tricks?

Check out TRICK TALK on page 32 for more information on these tricks.

(You will find information about PICTOGRAMS on page 28)

EXTREME HEROES

Matt says, 'Shane (Tasmanian Devil) Yost is a professional inline skater famous for his flips and spins. Shane was the first skater to pull a *1260* (that's 1260 degrees — three and a half full spins in mid-air).'

EXTREME HEROES

Laura says, 'Snowboarder Jussi Oksanen from Finland is fast becoming a hero to snowboarders everywhere. Jussi has a great style and he can spin *1080s* (that's 1080 **degrees** – three full spins) in both switchstance and his normal stance'.

EXTREME HEROES

Oli says, 'Tony Hawk is one of the world's most famous skateboarders. He has won hundreds of competitions and invented dozens of tricks. He turned professional when he was just 14 years old. Tony went into skateboarding history when he landed the first ever *900* (that's 900 degrees – two and a half mid-air turns) at the 1999 *X Games*.'

Tony Hawk pulls a 'gymnast plant'.

Laura Berry performing a 'frontside 540 melon'.

CHALLENGE QUESTIONS

How long do skates and boards last? Oli says, 'A skateboard belonging to a beginner could last for a year. But a board belonging to a **pro**, who is practising jumping down a set of 20 steps, might only last for an hour!'

These boards and skates have all been used for hours of tough practising. They are now worn out or damaged, and are no longer in use.

The inline skate wheels lasted: May and June

The snowboard lasted: 336 hours

The skateboard lasted: 10 080 minutes

a) How long did each last in days?
b) How long did each last in weeks?

(You will find a TIP to help you with these questions on page 28)

In speed skating competitions, inline skaters compete on flat or banked tracks and on roads that are closed down specially for the race. Top speed skaters compete in championship competitions, while skaters of all abilities can take part in *rat races*. During a race, skaters form pace lines (groups), where the competitors take it in turn to **slipstream** each other to conserve energy. Depending on their tactics, skaters will move from group to group, slowing down, then speeding up again throughout the race. As the end of the race approaches, the skaters will break from their groups, make their final moves and sprint for the finish line.

GO FOR IT!

Speed skaters compete over a variety of distances, from 300 metre sprint races to 50 kilometre marathons, and 161 kilometre endurance races.

A speed skating competition is being held on a track that is 130 metres long.
The competitors will race over these distances:
a) 500 m   b) 1000 m   c) 1500 m   d) 5000 m

1) Match these numbers of laps to the races above:

e) More than 11, but less than 12
f) More than 3, but less than 4
g) More than 38, but less than 39
h) More than 7, but less than 8

2) Which of the four races is closest to an exact number of laps?

Some races are being held on a track that is 400 metres long.

3. How many laps and **fractions** of a lap do competitors cover in the following races:

a) 500 m   b) 1000 m   c) 1500 m
d) 3000 m   e) 5000 m   f) 10 000 m

EXTREME HEROES

In September 2003, inline skater Jürgen Köhler set a new world inline speed record of 281.25 kilometres per hour. How did he do it? By wearing custom-built, speed skates, worth $8500, and by holding onto a Suzuki Hayabusa motorbike! Köhler had to make a number of attempts at reaching his record-breaking speed, and at one point, the Hayabusa actually caught fire! However, after a hard day's skating, a new record was achieved.

EXTREME HEROES

In 1998, two inline skaters, Dave Cooper and Eddy Matzger, put on their special off-road skates and actually skated up Mount Kilimanjaro, the highest mountain in Africa. It took them six days to roll up and two days to get back down. Their journey included skating through rainforest, over soft volcanic ash and into thick snow!

Speed skaters compete in a road race.

Mount Kilimanjaro, the highest mountain in Africa.

CHALLENGE QUESTIONS

US inline skater Debbie Rice holds the *Guinness world record* for being the fastest woman on skates. Debbie was clocked at a record-breaking speed of 61 mph (98 km/h).

A speed skater is trying to reach a speed of 60 mph.

a) How many miles is that in each minute?
b) How far is that per second:
   ⅙ mile, 0.5 mile, 0.6 mile, ¹⁄₆₀ mile?

EXTREME SLOPES

Sometimes only the highest, most dangerous slopes will do. In May 2001, 22 year old Marco Siffredi became the first person to snowboard down Mount Everest, the world's highest mountain peak. Marco and his support team climbed to the summit of Everest and then, at first light, Marco set off alone on his amazing downward journey. It took Marco just two and a half hours to snowboard down Everest. He used no special equipment, just his snowboard and his own tremendous skill and nerve. Sadly, some months later, while attempting to repeat this snowboarding feat, Marco disappeared. A sad end to an amazing extreme sports story.

GO FOR IT!

See if you can conquer these questions about extreme slopes and the world's highest mountains.

1) If Marco Siffredi snowboarded 8000 metres in 2 hours, how far did he snowboard in 1 hour?

2) So Marco's speed was ..... per hour.

3) Find the difference in heights between the mega mountains in the DATA BOX:

a) Mount McKinley and Vinson Massif
b) Everest and Aconcagua
c) Kilimanjaro and Elbrus
d) Aconcagua and Vinson Massif
e) Everest and Kilimanjaro

(You will find a TIP to help you with question 3 on page 29)

SNOWBOARD TALK

CARVE To weave back and forth, while going downhill.

WIND LIPS Natural jumps made from snow, blown into place by the wind.

HIT When a snowboarder pulls a trick in the air.

SNOWBOARDING FACT

In some of the world's most extreme places, such as Alaska, it is so difficult to get to the slopes, snowboarders have to be dropped on the mountain tops by helicopters.

MEGA MOUNTAINS

Here are some of the world's highest mountains. All of these mountains have been conquered by snowboarders!

| Asia: Mount Everest 8850 metres high | South America: Aconcagua 6960 metres high | North America: Mount McKinley 6194 metres high | Africa: Kilimanjaro 5895 metres high | Europe: Elbrus 5642 metres high | Antarctica: Vinson Massif 4897 metres high |

An extreme snowboarder riding off-piste.

CHALLENGE QUESTION

Snowboarding trails (routes that can be taken down a mountain) are given different ratings according to their level of difficulty. Snowboarders need to look out for these symbols.

The snowboard trail symbols are all symmetrical.

EASIEST RUN

MORE DIFFICULT

DIFFICULT

VERY DIFFICULT – use extreme caution

The green circle has an infinite number of **lines of symmetry**. How many lines of symmetry do the other two symbols have?

(You will find information about LINES OF SYMMETRY on page 29)

SNOWBOARDING FACT

Snowboarders have been killed by **avalanches**. When riding **off-piste**, snowboarders need to check the snow conditions to make sure there is no danger of an avalanche. They often carry small devices called transceivers. If snowboarders become trapped under an avalanche, the transceiver will give out a signal that can help rescue services find them.

In *vert competitions* skaters and skateboarders show what they can do on ramps, **halfpipes** and on boxes (huge plywood boxes with sloping sides). Skaters are not disqualified if they fall because it's all about going for the most difficult and exciting moves. The story goes that **vert skating** was invented one summer completely by accident. A young skateboarder drained his family's swimming pool so that he and his friends could roll down towards the deep end on their skateboards. The skaters soon realised that with enough speed they could actually ride up the walls of the swimming pool. A whole new range of skating possibilities opened up!

GO FOR IT!

Many skaters and skateboarders actually build ramps and boxes so that they can create skateparks in their own gardens!

A group of skaters have been busy building a ramp from plywood. Some wooden offcuts have been sorted out according to the shape of one of their faces.

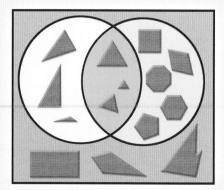

1) Can you tell how these offcuts have been sorted?

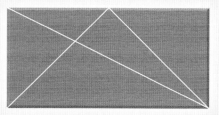

2) How many triangles can you find here?

(You will find a TIP to help you with question 1 on page 29)

Skaters wait on the platform to 'drop in'.

Vert area – this section goes straight up.

EXTREME HEROES

UK skateboarders, Joel and Paul Spaven and Jamie Manby have built the world's longest skateboard. The giant board is 7.21 metres (23.65 ft) long, 30 centimetres (11.81 in) wide and 7.5 centimetres (2.95 in) thick. It cost £500 to build.

Transition

A tail grab

VERT SKATING TALK

HALFPIPE A U-shaped ramp with a flat section in the middle. When viewed from the side it looks like a giant pipe cut in half. The vertical, or *vert*, area at the top, stops the skaters drifting away from the ramp when they launch into air tricks.

MINI RAMP A small halfpipe 1 to 1.8 metres high, but with no *vert* area.

QUARTERPIPE One half of a mini-ramp or a quarter of a pipe if viewed from the side. Quarterpipes are usually found in the street area at skateparks.

BOWLS Giant bowl-shaped areas in the ground. Bowls are normally found at outdoor parks and are made from concrete.

CHALLENGE QUESTIONS

Here are the plans for a ramp. The plans show the length, width and height of the ramp.

a) What is the **area** of the ramp's surface approximately?
b) What is the **perimeter** of the ramp's surface approximately?

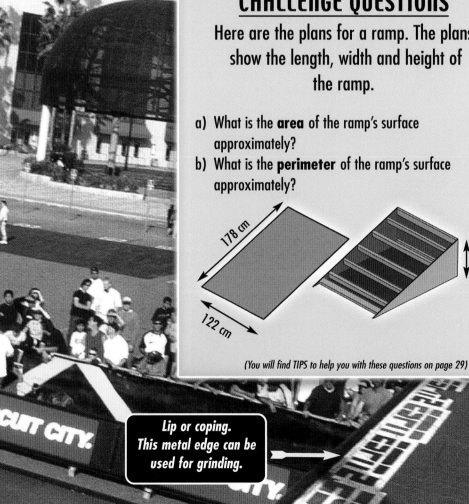

178 cm

122 cm

59 cm

(You will find TIPS to help you with these questions on page 29)

Flat area

**Lip or coping.
This metal edge can be used for grinding.**

O li and Matt say, '**Street skating** is now illegal in a lot of public places. Many towns and cities around the world have passed laws that ban this type of skating because it can cause damage to railings, curbs, steps and park benches. Skateparks offer a safe and legal way for skaters and skateboarders to enjoy their sport without getting into trouble! They are also a great place to show off all your best moves and meet up with your friends.' Laura says, 'Indoor snowboarding facilities mean snowboarders can ride and practise their tricks all year round — even if it's hot and sunny outside.'

GO FOR IT!

A new extreme sports centre has just opened. Some skaters and boarders are checking out the equipment shop and snack bar.

1) Tickets to go into the new centre cost £6. With £38, how many tickets could you buy?

2) A meal in the snack bar is £3.99. How many meals can be bought with £20?

3) Tubes of *shoegoo* are packed in boxes of 70 tubes. If $\frac{2}{7}$ of a box is sold, how many tubes are left? If 214 tubes are sold, how many boxes will need to be opened?

4. There are 506 pairs of knee pads in stock, 52 of which are on display. Half of the knee pads not on display are sent to another sports centre shop. How many pairs is that?

5. Badges are displayed on cards. There are 60 badges on each card. How many rows of badges will there be on a card if the badges are arranged in rows of **10, 5, 20, 3, 12?**

(You will find a TIP to help you with question 2 on page 29)

SKATE TALK

JAM Getting a load of **aggressive skaters** or skateboarders together for a skating *session*.

SESSION The act of skateboarding or inline skating. For example, you can *session a ramp* or *have a street session*.

THRASHED or WRECKED The wear and tear on an object due to skateboarding or skating.

WALLIE Skating onto, up and over a street object.

WALLRIDE Skating up a vertical wall.

STOKED The feeling of doing something well.

SNOWBOARDING FACT

Snowboarding as we see it today was started in 1965. A guy called Sherman Poppen, from Michigan, USA, screwed two skis together to create, what he called, a *snurfer*. He created this name from the words *snow* and *surfer*.

GEAR GUIDE

IMPACT SHORTS Snowboarders often wear these to provide protection for their hips and lower back. The shorts contain thick padding.

SHOES Skateboarding can cause some serious wear and tear on your shoes. You can buy special skateboarding shoes with ultra-thick rubber soles or use *shoegoo* on your normal trainers.

SHOEGOO This liquid rubber can be put over holes in your shoes or used to rebuild the soles. Spread it on and watch it go hard!

SKATE JEANS Wide and baggy jeans which give you plenty of room for your knee and shin pads. The bottoms are wide enough to drop over your skates. The jeans can contain removable padding.

CHALLENGE QUESTIONS

A survey is done during the first hour that the new extreme sports centre is open. The results are entered on a *tally chart*.

LOCATION IN THE CENTRE	NUMBER OF PEOPLE
Spectator area	𝍸 𝍸 𝍸 𝍸 𝍸 II
Snowboarding area	𝍸 𝍸 𝍸 𝍸 𝍸 𝍸 𝍸 III
Street course	𝍸 𝍸 𝍸 𝍸 𝍸 𝍸 𝍸 𝍸 𝍸 𝍸 I
Vert ramps	𝍸 𝍸 𝍸 IIII
Snack bar	𝍸 𝍸 𝍸 𝍸 𝍸 II
Equipment shop	𝍸 𝍸 𝍸 𝍸
Amusement arcade	𝍸 𝍸 I

a) Which facility is least popular?

b) What is the difference in the number of people who are snowboarding compared with those who are **vert skating**?

c) How many people are taking part in extreme sports altogether?

d) If 15 more people go for a snack, what will the new snack bar total be?

(You will find information about TALLY CHARTS on page 29)

Laura Berry rides a rail at an indoor snowboarding centre.

EXTREME SPORTS CHALLENGE

The world's top extreme athletes get plenty of chances to meet up and compete against each other. Snowboarders compete in the Winter Olympics, and skaters and skateboarders take part in competitions such as the *X Games* and the *Gravity Games*. At the *X Games*, the winning skaters take home cash prizes and medals. Skating and boarding companies usually have a team of around ten or twenty boarders or skaters who, as part of their deal with the company, take part in competitions and demonstrations around the world. On these pages you will see snowboarders, skaters and skateboarders who are showcasing their skills in the EXTREME SPORTS CHALLENGE.

GO FOR IT!

Each of the competitors are working hard to impress the crowds and grab the judges' attention!

1) The most steps a skateboarder has cleared so far today is seven. Jez takes off and clears three times that many. How many steps has Jez jumped?

2) Ed is trying to land a *900*. He falls 9 times, but lands the trick 3 times. Show Ed's successes as a **fraction** of his tota number of attempts. Then show your answer as a **decimal fraction**.

3) Cal has just achieved an **amplitude** of 821 centimetres in the *Big Air competition*. How much higher does he need to jump to reach the *highest air* record of 9 metres?

4) Charlie has been awarded the following points on her street run: 44, 15, 9 and 28. Use Charlie's scores to make as many addition and subtraction statements as you can.

Judges in sports competitions need to be able to order numbers.

5) Can you place these decimal fractions where they go on the number line?   0.7, 0.2, 1.3, 1.9, 0.6, 1.5, 1.1, 0.8

(You will find information about NUMBER LINES on page 29)

SKATEBOARDING FACT

Street luge is STRICTLY for the **pros**. Riders lay flat on their backs on special, extra long skateboards. They hurtle downhill on twisting, turning courses at speeds of up to 113 km/h. Street lugers wear full-body, leather suits and motorcycle helmets. They also wear rubber-soled shoes because they use their feet to brake!

Charlie

Cal

Ed

Matt

Laura

CHALLENGE QUESTIONS

Snow sports need low temperatures. Remember, when it gets below freezing, we use negative numbers on the Celsius scale.
Look at the thermometer:

a) The temperature rises by 5 **degrees**. What is the new temperature?

b) If the temperature is −5°C and rises to 8°C, how much warmer has it become?

c) The temperature starts out at freezing. It rises 9° during the day and then drops 11° at night. What is the night time temperature?

TIPS FOR MATHS SUCCESS

PAGES 6-7

GO FOR IT!

Interpreting a bar chart:

Bar charts have bars that should always be the same width. It is the heights of the bars that allow you to compare things. In a bar chart, you need to know what each bar stands for and what the scale is. *For example, is the scale going up in 1s, 2s, 5s, 10s, 100s, 1000s or some other amount?*

CHALLENGE QUESTIONS

Rounding whole numbers and decimal fractions:

When rounding whole numbers and **decimal fractions**, we always follow the same rules:
36 rounded to the nearest ten is 40 because we round up numbers that end in 5, 6, 7, 8 or 9. We round down numbers that end in 4, 3, 2 or 1.
For example, 32 would be rounded down to 30.
When rounding decimal fractions to the nearest whole number, we use the same rules:
so 3.6 is rounded up to 4 and 3.2 is rounded down to 3.

PAGES 8-9

Making turns and measuring angles:

An **angle** is a measure of turn. Angles are measured in **degrees**. The symbol for degrees is °.
One whole turn (a complete revolution) is 360°.
A quarter turn is 90°, or one *right angle*. There are four *right angles* in one whole turn.

PAGES 10-11

GO FOR IT!

Ordering numbers:

When we put things in order 1st, 2nd, 3rd, 4th and so on, we are using *ordinal numbers*. Counting numbers 1, 2, 3, 4 and so on, are called *cardinal numbers*.

CHALLENGE QUESTION

TIP: One foot is about 30 centimetres.

PAGES 12-13

GO FOR IT!

TIPS: When adding (summing) several small numbers:
- See if you can begin with the largest number.
- Look for pairs to make ten.
- Find numbers appearing more than once so that you can use multiplication tables.

For example, 7 + 7 + 7 is the same as 3 x 7.

CHALLENGE QUESTION

Interpreting a bar line graph:

The chart in this section is known as a *bar line graph*. Use a ruler or pencil to check and compare the heights of the bar lines in the chart.

Sometimes we can connect the tops of the lines in a bar line graph to make a continuous line graph. The tops of the bar lines here cannot be joined because the bits of information are separate from one another. Joining one person's *big air jump* height to another's, makes no sense.

PAGES 14-15

GO FOR IT!

Using data in a pictogram:

A **pictogram** is a chart where a picture is used to show several units. In the pictogram on page 14, a picture of a complete wheel or snowflake stands for practising a trick 10 times. Pictures can be cut into **fractions** so each of these half pictures show 5 times.

CHALLENGE QUESTIONS

TIP: There are —
- 60 minutes in one hour.
- 24 hours in one day.
- 7 days in one week.
- 4-5 weeks in one month.

You can use a calendar to find out exactly how many days there are in each of the 12 months of the year.

PAGES 20–21

GO FOR IT!

Writing down calculations:

When using large numbers, you can set out the calculation down the page to help with the working out. Remember to line up the numbers so that the thousands go under the thousands and so on. Look at these examples:

```
   2285        9785
  +4193       –2315
   6478        7470
```

CHALLENGE QUESTION

TIP: If a shape can be cut in half so that the halves match, we say that it has a **line of symmetry**. Wherever you cut a circle, so long as you go through the centre, your cut will be along a line of symmetry.

PAGES 22–23

GO FOR IT!

Using sorting diagrams to display information about shapes:

This type of diagram is called a *Venn diagram*. In this example, the sets of shapes intersect (overlap).

TIP: **2-D** shapes with three or more sides are called *polygons*. A regular 2-D shape has all sides the same length.

CHALLENGE QUESTIONS

Measuring the area and perimeter of rectangles:
TIP: To find the **area** of a rectangle you need to multiply the length and the width.

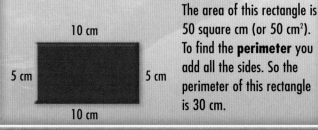

10 cm

5 cm   5 cm

10 cm

The area of this rectangle is 50 square cm (or 50 cm²). To find the **perimeter** you add all the sides. So the perimeter of this rectangle is 30 cm.

PAGES 24–25

GO FOR IT!

TIP: When doing shopping calculations you can round up prices to work out approximate amounts. So £3.99 can be rounded to £4 to make mental work easier. Don't forget to take away 1p off the £4 to get the answer at the end.

CHALLENGE QUESTIONS

Using data in a tally chart:

A *tally chart* is a quick way of recording or counting the amount of something. One of something is shown as one *tally mark* 'I'. The fifth line is drawn across the first four (IIII) to make five lines in total. Use your knowledge of the products of the x5 table to quickly add when using *tally marks*.

PAGES 26–27

GO FOR IT!

Number lines:
A number line is continuous and extends forever in both directions.

$$-5 \quad -4 \quad -3 \quad -2 \quad -1 \quad 0 \quad 1 \quad 2 \quad 3 \quad 4 \quad 5$$

UNITS OF MEASUREMENT

We use two systems of measurement in the UK: *metric* (centimetres, metres, kilometres, grams, kilograms) and *imperial* (inches, feet, miles, ounces, pounds).

METRIC		IMPERIAL	
Length		**Length**	
1 millimetre (mm)		1 inch (in)	
1 centimetre (cm)	= 10 mm	1 foot (ft)	= 12 in
1 metre (m)	= 100 cm	1 yard (yd)	= 3 ft
1 kilometre (km)	= 1000 m	1 mile	= 1760 yd
Weight		**Weight**	
1 gram (g)		1 ounce (oz)	
1 kilogram (kg)	= 1000 g	1 pound (lb)	= 16 oz
Capacity		**Capacity**	
1 millilitre (ml)		1 fluid ounce (fl oz)	
1 litre (l)	= 1000 ml	1 UK pint (pt)	= 20 fl oz

Comparing metric and imperial measurements:

1 kilometre = 0.62 of a mile   1 kilogram = 2.2 pounds

0.57 litre = 1 UK pint

ANSWERS ANSWERS

GO FOR IT!

1) Slightly more than 120 (122)
2) About 200 people.
3) Slightly more than 10 + 5 (12 + 5 = 17)
4) The total number of people questioned can be found out from the **bar chart**.

CHALLENGE QUESTIONS

a) Board A offers the biggest **range**: 15 cm.
b) Board B is £350 when rounded to the nearest ten pounds.

GO FOR IT!

Trick 1) The skateboarder made a ¼ turn which is 90°.
Trick 2) The skateboarder made a ½ turn which is 180°.
Trick 3) The skateboarder made a whole turn which is 360°.

CHALLENGE QUESTIONS

a) 45°   b) 60°   c) 30°   d) 270°

GO FOR IT!

1) 5 skaters had a time under 26 seconds.
2) Josh, Ant and Dave had a time over 27 seconds.
3) If another skater finished the sprint in 25.3 seconds, he would be ranked 5th.
4) • At TRACK A there will be 21 races.
   • At TRACK B there will be 10 races.
   • At TRACK C there will be 17 races.

CHALLENGE QUESTION

The height of the jump is approximately 13 feet.

GO FOR IT!

1) Alli got the lowest total score.
2) Zak did better than Rob in both **amplitude** and overall impression.
3) Rob got the same score as Zak.
4) Three people – Rob (31), Zak (31) and Alli (23).
5) Laura won the competition with 32 points.

CHALLENGE QUESTIONS

a) The **range** of heights jumped was 1.6 metres.
b) The *mode* (most common height of jump) was 4.2 metres.

GO FOR IT!

1) Trick 'a' was practised:
   SKATEBOARDER: *Kickflip* 40 times
   INLINE SKATER: *Mute air* 60 times
   SNOWBOARDER: *Rodeo* 100 times

2)   SKATEBOARDER: *Kickflips* were practised 15 more times than *50-50 grinds*.
   INLINE SKATER: *Mute airs* were practised 10 more times than *Lui Kangs*.
   SNOWBOARDER: *Rodeos* were practised 35 more times than *frontside 540 melons*.

3)   SKATEBOARDER: 135 times
   INLINE SKATER: 175 times
   SNOWBOARDER: 180 times

CHALLENGE QUESTIONS

a) • The inline skate wheels lasted 61 days.
   • The snowboard lasted 14 days.
   • The skateboard lasted 7 days (168 hours).
b) • The inline skate wheels lasted 8 weeks and 5 days.
   • The snowboard lasted 2 weeks.
   • The skateboard lasted 1 week.

PAGES 16–17

GO FOR IT!

Route 1:	20	Route 2:	10
Route 3:	90	Route 4:	11
Route 5:	18	Route 6:	50

CHALLENGE QUESTION

The shop would sell 510 skateboards.

PAGES 18–19

GO FOR IT!

1) e and c / f and a / g and d/ h and b
2) Race 'a' 500 m (race a is just under 4 laps, race b is just over 7½ laps, races c and d are nearly 11½ and 38½ laps respectively.)
3)　　a) 1¼ laps　　b) 2 ½ laps　　c) 3 ¾ laps
　　　d) 7 ½ laps　　e) 12 ½ laps　　f) 25 laps

CHALLENGE QUESTIONS

a) 1 mile in each minute.
b) ¹⁄₆₀ mile per second.

PAGES 20–21

GO FOR IT!

1) 4000 metres
2) 4000 m per hour or 4 km/h.

3)
a) McKinley and Vinson Massif	b) Everest and Aconcagua	c) Kilimanjaro and Elbrus
6194	8850	5895
− 4897	− 6960	− 5642
1297 metres	1890 metres	253 metres

d) Aconcagua and Vinson Massif	e) Everest and Kilimanjaro
6960	8850
− 4897	− 5895
2063 metres	2955 metres

CHALLENGE QUESTION

A square has 4 **lines of** symmetry.

A rhombus has 2 lines of symmetry.

PAGES 22–23

GO FOR IT!

1) The offcuts were sorted into the following sets:

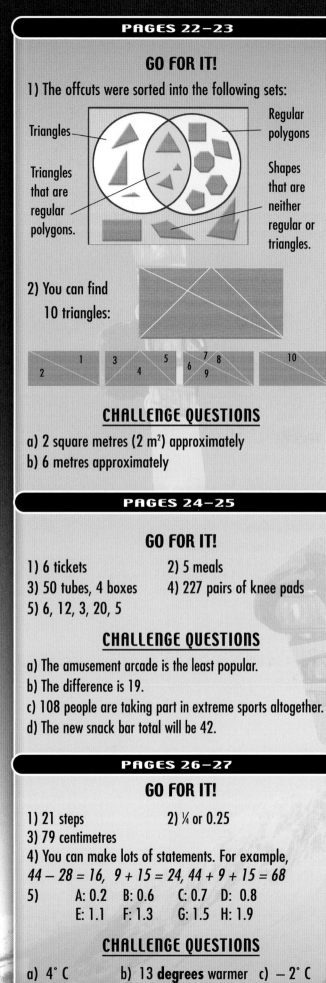

Triangles

Triangles that are regular polygons.

Regular polygons

Shapes that are neither regular or triangles.

2) You can find 10 triangles:

CHALLENGE QUESTIONS

a) 2 square metres (2 m²) approximately
b) 6 metres approximately

PAGES 24–25

GO FOR IT!

1) 6 tickets　　　　2) 5 meals
3) 50 tubes, 4 boxes　　4) 227 pairs of knee pads
5) 6, 12, 3, 20, 5

CHALLENGE QUESTIONS

a) The amusement arcade is the least popular.
b) The difference is 19.
c) 108 people are taking part in extreme sports altogether.
d) The new snack bar total will be 42.

PAGES 26–27

GO FOR IT!

1) 21 steps　　　　　　2) ¼ or 0.25
3) 79 centimetres
4) You can make lots of statements. For example,
$44 − 28 = 16,\ 9 + 15 = 24,\ 44 + 9 + 15 = 68$
5)　　A: 0.2　B: 0.6　　C: 0.7　D: 0.8
　　　E: 1.1　F: 1.3　　G: 1.5　H: 1.9

CHALLENGE QUESTIONS

a) 4° C　　　　b) 13 **degrees** warmer　c) − 2° C

GLOSSARY

ADRENALINE A chemical produced in your body. It increases your heart rate and blood pressure, making you feel a rush of excitement or fear.

AGGRESSIVE SKATERS Inline skaters who perform tricks, such as airs, spins, flips and grabs, on ramps and pipes or over street obstacles.

AMPLITUDE The height a snowboarder jumps above the lip of a halfpipe.

AVALANCHES Large masses of snow that break loose and move down the side of a mountain.

BACKSIDE Moving or jumping with your back facing the direction you are travelling in. The opposite to *frontside*.

HALFPIPES U-shaped ramps (normally made from wood) that when viewed from the side look like giant pipes cut in half. Skateboarders and inline skaters use them for vert skating. In snowboarding, halfpipes are like long pipes that have been cut in half. They are made of snow.

OFF-PISTE Snowboarding on a mountain slope that has not been prepared for skiing or snowboarding.

PROS (Professionals) Skaters, skateboarders or snowboarders who are paid to take part in their sport.

SLIPSTREAM Using the stream of air created by the person in front of you to pull you along.

STREET SKATING Using everyday items such as curbs, park benches, stairs and handrails to perform tricks.

VERT SKATING Using bowls, ramps and halfpipes to perform tricks and gain height. *Vert* is short for vertical.

TRICK TALK

SKATEBOARDING

KICKFLIP While you are in the air, you kick down on the front of your board and spin it around underneath you.

50-50 GRIND Start parallel to an obstacle such as a curb or a rail. *Ollie* onto the obstacle so both trucks (axles) grind against it, then jump off.

BOARDSLIDE Like a grind, but your board is at 90° to the obstacle, with the middle of your board grinding along the obstacle.

SNOWBOARDING

RODEO You do a full back flip in the air while spinning 540°.

540 MELON One and a half spins, while grabbing the board between your legs at the back with your front hand.

BACKSIDE 180 INDY If you are goofy, you spin 180° anti-clockwise, while grabbing the board with your back hand between your legs, at the front.

MATHS GLOSSARY

2-D (TWO DIMENSIONAL) Flat with length (or height) and width, but no depth (thickness).

ANGLE A measure of turn.

AREA The measure of the size of a surface, made in squares (all of the same size).

BAR CHART A chart with bars of the same width that can be used to compare numbers of things against a scale.

DECIMAL FRACTIONS We use a counting system involving tens, multiples of ten and fractions of ten. The decimal point separates whole numbers from decimal fractions. *For example, in the number 672.53, 5 is tenths and 3 is hundredths.*

DEGREES The units used for measuring angles and temperatures.

ESTIMATE To find a number or amount that is close to an exact answer.

FRACTIONS These are made when shapes or numbers are cut into equal parts. For example, if a shape is cut into four equal parts, each part is one whole divided by four, or a quarter (¼).

LINE OF SYMMETRY A line dividing a shape into two matching halves.

PERIMETER The distance all the way around a shape.

PICTOGRAM In a pictogram pictures are used to show information.

RANGE The difference between the highest and the lowest values.

t=top, b=bottom, c=centre, l=left, r=right, OFC=outside front cover, OBC=outside back cover
Alamy: OFC, 2-3, 6cr, 7bl, 8-9, 10-11, 12, 14-15main, 17t, 17br, 18-19main, 20-21main, 24-25t, 26cr, 26-27c, 27tl, 27tr, 27cr, OBC.
Anna Bond (Matt King): 1. Corbis: 19tr. TheBoarder.co.uk: 6-7main, 15b, 27bl.
The Friedman Archives (Gary Friedman): 17c, 22-23. www.dopeshots.com: 24-25b.
Every effort has been made to trace the copyright holders, and we apologize in advance for any unintentional omissions.
We would be pleased to insert the appropriate acknowledgements in any subsequent edition of this publication.